Taking the GOO Out of Google Local

17 Secrets

Directly From Google
to **Triple**
or Even **QUADRUPLE**
Your **MONEY**
with **Your** Google Local Listing

Plus…

5 Amazing Tips

For Responding
To Negative Reviews
REVEALED

STEVE J HUSKEY

Do you want better results from Google?

I'll show you how to create a remarkably successful, money-making Google Local listing - to 100% completeness - so you can *beat your competitors*.

Dear Soon-to-Be-Millionaire:

Have you ever seen a magician pull a rabbit out of a hat? A knife thrower hurl razor sharp daggers at his beautiful blindfolded assistant? A snake charmer and a cobra swaying back and forth, as the charmer leans within striking range of the snakes deadly fangs? These tricks are shocking. But the truth is, if someone showed you how to do it, you could do it too. Creating an effective Google Local listing is easy.

Wrong, Wrong, Wrong!

That's how I describe the majority of the Google Local listings that I see. It's <u>spam</u>. Not worth the money that was invested into it.

Data from Google shows that upwards of 85% of Google Local (a.k.a. Google Places or Google Maps) listings are not structured so that Google's computers can read them. Many times these listings get categorized as spam. These simple oversights can be costing you thousands.

Invest a few tax-deductible dollars in this book.

- **You will make more money** as a result of a listing that is 100% complete.
- Your listing will **be shown in front of your competitors**.
- Google will be able to read your listing **so it will show up in results with more frequency**.
- Your listing will **be featured on page 1**.

In these easy-to-read pages, I equip you with methodologies that can make your listing show up in front of your competitors. I teach you how to turn dismal, useless listings into Google-friendly, powerful money-makers that help boost your rankings *fast*. No special talents are necessary. These methods cost nothing. Once you read the tips, it will be easy.

Above all, if you suffer from not having the knowledge or desire - as most business owners do today – this book will show you how to Take the Goo out of Google and improve your Google Local ranking.

Ready to dig in? Let's go!

Steve Huskey
StevenHuskey@gmail.com
Twitter: @WizardOfGoogle
Website: http://www.GooOutOfGoogle.com

PS – After reading this book, if you still need help, I also offer instructional videos on my website that walk you through step by step.

Dedications

For my Dad. You encouraged my growth in computers beginning in 4th Grade. You helped me build my first radio. You bought me a computer to practice programming at home. Your encouragement has led to a lifelong interest in technology.

I am especially grateful to my wonderful wife, Shawna. You have always been patient with my new ideas.

Thank You.

Table of Contents

Table of Contents ....

17-Point Quick Reference Guide ....

Icons Used In This Book ....

Introduction ....
    Google Wants to do Business With You 11
    The Phone Book is Dead! 12
    Give Google 100% of Your Business 13
    Don't Give Up 14
    What Your Setup Screen Looks Like 16

Basic Information ....

Description ....

Categories ....

Service Areas and Location Settings ....
    How to Hide Your Address if You Work From home 24

Hours of Operation ....
    You Are Always Open 26

Payment Options ....
    Your Listing is Almost 100% Complete 27

Photos and Videos ....

Additional Details ....

Reviews ....

Responding to Negative Reviews Easy ....
    5-Point Checklist for Responding to Reviews 35

Duplicate Pages ....

Troubleshooting 38

   My listing is not showing as frequently as I would like. **38**

   My page is not showing. What can I do to get into the rotation more? **38**

   My map marker is not in the correct place **39**

   I did everything you said and I'm still not showing **39**

   I get an error saying, "We Currently Do Not Support the Location" **39**

Closing 41

17-Point Quick Reference Guide

1. You will need your username (email address) and password for Google.
2. What is the website URL that you would like to link with your listing?
3. In 2 – 3 sentences, what makes your business unique? Is it 24/7 service? Quality of work? Or something else? This is your description.
4. Include your five most lucrative services in the category fields.
5. Use your company name on your business license or the sign outside your door.
6. What country are you in?
7. You will need to provide the address, within the service area, where you receive mail.
8. How often do customers come to your business? If never, then do not list an address.
9. If so, what is your physical address?
10. Include your main business phone number.
11. What is your main business email address?
12. What are the limits of your service areas? The northern-most, southern-most, eastern-most, and western-most service areas?
13. What are your hours of operation?
14. List all forms of payment that you accept.
15. Include 10 photos. Photos of you and your staff will help soften your page.
16. If you have videos on YouTube, feel free to link to one of those. If not, write down your 5 FAQ's, video those, list them on YouTube, and then link to them.
17. Is your map marker in the right place? Be sure to view both views: map and satellite.

Icons Used In This Book

 It is in your best interest to pay attention to this icon. This icon will alert you to items that are particularly important.

 This icon is being used to signal information that you may want to write down for future reference

 This icon gives you Google-approved advice.

Introduction

This is a business altering book. It will show you how to use Google Local to get more traffic to your website. I am not exaggerating for effect. It is an absolute guarantee that if you will read these principles, understand them, and then apply them, it will change your business in a fundamental way – for good.

Your business will have an improved public image. You will have more customers to harvest. You will be in more control of your future. Using these principles will significantly improve the quality of relationships with your customers. It will also improve the quantity of quality customers that find you. You can expect it, it will happen. Once your listing gets ranked higher and your business gets noticed more, your capacity to inspire and persuade others will be enhanced. You will experience growth, learning, increased self-respect, self-confidence, and happiness. You can expect both dramatic and progressive results. This is an evolution not a revolution. This is not based on a fad or technique.

To make things increasingly easy, this book has been organized to follow a Google Local listing setup from creation to completion. Once you complete a step with your online listing, simply turn the page in the book and you will be taken to the next step in the creation process. First, I will set expectations for how long this will take you from start to finish. I call it Google-time. It will be more closely defined in later chapters. Next, the setup is written in order for easy reference. We will set it up according to how Google wants an effective listing to read. As quickly as you can turn the page, you can setup your listing. Finally, we go through trouble shooting common issues and their fixes.

Don't forget to pay attention to the notification icons. There are three icons that highlight particularly important pieces of information. Simply paying attention to these will increase the visibility of your page.

This book is a compilation of the presentations I have attended, my continuing education online, and real work experiences as a professional internet marketing consultant. What I learned was that it is Google's interpretation of our listing that affects our ranking.

These methodologies apply as much to large businesses as they do to small businesses, not for profits, startups, private businesses, and Fortune 500 companies. They are like common denominators. They are principles that apply to everyone using Google.

Most people tend to want a quick fix. Many online marketing professionals give quick promises of relief. The difficulty is they work on acute issues or problems without looking at the big picture. They want the pain to be relieved so that relationship can be instantly resolved. They are into tricks. The more you try to apply a gimmick or quick fix, the worse your problems may become.

These methodologies address the chronic problems and expose opportunities.

Google Wants to do Business With You

When was the last time you got something for free? Every time you use Google, you are using a free service. Google doesn't own much of what you want. They are the broker for what you want.

Google's mission statement reads, "To organize the world's information and make it universally accessible and useful." To do this they count on you the business owner to help them out. It is in your best interest to list your business, but its also in Google's best interest that you list your information. So be patient and know they are just as enthusiastic to have your information indexed as you are. They want to broker the information. They just want to check your credentials and credibility first.

Speaking of brokers, if you have used a broker for free, how was the quality of their work? Likely if their service was free, you got what you paid for. Did they let you use their service for free again and again, as often as you liked?

Google strives to give you the most recent, relevant information that you are looking for. This is so much more than a phone book. It is an encyclopedia, almanac, map, meteorologist, email service, video database, and all around information broker. It does all of these things repeatedly for free. Best of all, they are constantly striving to serve you better.

One of the ways they do this is by using something they call Quality Score. It's Google's way of separating websites that are relevant to your search term from those that are not. The factors include, website quality, website load time, and how often people click on your listing when it is shown, (a.k.a. click through rate).

Google monitors quality score with special software robots that crawl the web looking for new information. These are also called spiders. By taking note of the words on a page and where they were found, Google is able to assign a site a quality score. This, in turn, helps them show you a relevant result. By showing you a more relevant result on your first try, the idea is that you'll come back to Google to search again.

The Phone Book is Dead!

Google Local (a.k.a. Google Places or Google Maps) connects searchers with relevant local listings on the map. Google's annual report says they have more than 50 million maps listings worldwide.

This service has proven so popular that it is now featured in the top right corner of most searches. When people want to find a local business, it is faster and easier than ever to see how far they are from a business using the map. Surfers can see details about your business including pictures and videos. Best of all, it's free!

There is no reason why your business should not be on the first page of Google…unless you're not interested in profitability. They want you to be there. They will list you for free *if* you follow their rules. Rule #1, have your page filled out entirely - 100%. Getting to 100% is a matter of filling out all of the information in the format Google wants, having at least two photos, and a video. You will have to avoid running into a category spam filter, how to use keywords to increase engagement of your listing, but I can show you all of that.

Rule #2, Google wants fresh and relevant information for its users. It is important to keep your page fresh with new content. Content consists of pictures, videos, reviews, etc… Keep it fresh every 30 days-ish.

Bottom line: Complete the steps in this book and you will make more money.

Give Google 100% of Your Business

What do you mean give Google 100% of my business? Are you crazy? I am a firm believer in taking the path of least resistance with Google. If you want to be liked by Google, you must work with them - on their terms. Again, Google is a huge public company. They are not required to list your business in their database. Therefore, following what they say to the precise word will pay dividends; your listing will be shown more often, for more keywords, and in better placement. Failing to follow this, will most likely get your page marked as spam and largely delisted from Google. More on this spam later.

Unless you are an Internet marketing manager, you may not have noticed Google Places, formerly Google Maps, is now Google Local. Though, in the setup, Google still mentions "my maps listing". Gone is the 1 – 5 star review method. They found that the 5 star review system didn't work well across all industries. Google has adopted a Zagat-esque method of reviews, which gives options to select between 0 and 3 stars. The review is then multiplied by 10 to give a maximum score of 30. For example, now you can rank more than just your experience. You can also choose between Food, Décor, Services, Cost, etc… This gives people a better idea of what to expect when they do business with you.

Further changes have integrated Google Local with Menu.com and OpenTable.com for reservations and menus respectively. Imagine browsing a new restaurant on Google Local from your couch. You're now able to look at the menu and reserve a table with help from the Google Local interface.

Do you want to know how to get more 30-point reviews? Stay tuned. We will cover that in detail later in the book.

Don't Give Up

One of the major frustrations that I hear from customers is the timeframe in making changes. Remember that Google is a massive public company. They can do what they want. If you want to be seen on Google, you must remember that you are not dealing with a standardized time zone. You are effectively progressing on Google time.

Google does not push out all the information it has in real time. Google time does not work on a 24-hour clock; it functions through periodic index pushes. Often times an index push will take 3 – 4 weeks before a server will be refreshed. If your changes have taken more than 45 days, then it might be time to redo the changes. Essentially, this "pokes" Google in asking for an update. However, Google's own literature will tell you that they can take up to 30 days to process any changes. When you add that to a potential 3-week lag time for an index push, you could easily be looking at 51 days of turnaround time.

If you think that 51 days is a long time, then I urge you to look into a Search Engine Optimization campaign (SEO). Search Engine Optimization, if done effectively and properly will take several months to build proper momentum. It will likely cost you and arm or a leg or both. Google Local listings may take 50-90 days to get anointed by Google as legit, but they're free. Furthermore, SEO is constantly changing. Google is trying to weed out companies that are relevant from those that are trying to appear relevant. In doing so the SEO games are always evolving.

So stick with your Google Local listing. It will bring more customers to your business once it's 100% complete.

GOO OUT OF GOOGLE

What Your Setup Screen Looks Like

▼ Basic Information

Please note that changing your address or business name will require additional verification via mail or phone.

* Required Fields

Country: * United States

Company/Organization: *

Street Address: *

City/Town: *

State: * Select state

ZIP: * [?]

Main phone: *
Example: (201) 234-5678. Add more phone numbers

Email address:
Example: myname@example.com

Website:
Example: http://www.example.com
☐ I don't have a website

Description:
200 characters max. 200 characters left

Category: *
Which categories (up to 5) best describe your business?
Ex: Dentist, Wedding Photographer, Thai Restaurant
Add another category

©2012 Google - Terms of Use
Fix incorrect marker location

▼ Service Areas and Location Settings

Does your business provide services, such as delivery or home repair, to locations in a certain area?

◉ No, all customers come to the business location
○ Yes, this business serves customers at their locations

▼ Hours of operations

Make sure your customers know when you're open!

◉ I prefer not to specify operating hours.
○ My operating hours are:

Mon:	9:00 AM - 5:00 PM	☐ Closed	⇩ Apply to all
Tue:	9:00 AM - 5:00 PM	☐ Closed	
Wed:	9:00 AM - 5:00 PM	☐ Closed	
Thu:	9:00 AM - 5:00 PM	☐ Closed	
Fri:	9:00 AM - 5:00 PM	☐ Closed	
Sat:		☑ Closed	
Sun:		☑ Closed	

...r hours split during a single day, such as 9-11am *and* 7-10pm?
...like to enter two sets of hours for a single day.

...yment options

...how customers can pay at your business

- ...sh
- ...eck
- ...veler's Check
- ...oice
- [ ] American Express
- [ ] Diner's Club
- [ ] Discover
- [ ] MasterCard
- [ ] Visa
- [ ] Financing
- [ ] Google Checkout
- [ ] Paypal

...otos

...r to your listing: include photos of your products or your storefront. You can ...up to 10 photos. Please be sure they comply with our photo submission ...es.

...dd a photo from your computer

[Browse...] [**Add Photo**]

"Browse..." to choose a file from your computer

...dd a photo from the web

...ve uploaded **0** of up to **10** images for this listing.

...deos

...ce your listing by associating videos about your business. To do so, upload ...deo on YouTube and enter the URL below. You can include up to 5 videos.

[**Add Video**]

...ple http://youtube.com/watch?v=dFtfxv1JdXl

...ve uploaded **0** of up to **5** videos for this listing

...dditional Details

...e enter in any other details you want customers to know about your ...ss, for example:

...g available: Yes.
...s carried: Sony, Panasonic and Toshiba.

Add another

[Submit]

Basic Information

If you have a Gmail or a Google account, then your best bet is to log-in with that. You can use that Gmail or Google account as your Google Local account. If you do not have a Gmail or a Google account, then go set up a Gmail account.

Go to www.Gmail.com and click "set up a new Gmail account". You do not ever have to actually use it as an email, but that can be your Google log-in. Next, log-in with your email address. It will take you to www.google.com/places. Scroll down until you see "Get your business found on Google". Now click "Get started." It will ask you to log-in with your Google account.

If you DO NOT already have a Google Local page associated with the account, the setup interface will bring you to a separate window. If you DO have a Google Local page associated with that email, it is going to bring you directly to the Google Local dashboard.

Attention At this point you should ensure that there has not already been a Google Local page that was automatically created for you. Just because you did not create it does not mean that it has not already been created for you.

To look for your page, try typing in your business phone number. If there is a Google Local page under that phone number, then a Google Local page was already created for this. Now click the "Edit" button. It is going to allow you to edit that information then submit and verify it. In the instance that you have lost the log-in information for your Google account, you can log-in with the Gmail account that you just created. Unfortunately, you will have to put in the business phone number, and then click the "Edit" button. Then you must go through the verification process yet again. This is Google's way of securely transferring the ownership from the old page to the new page. The bottom line is, clicking the "Edit" button will walk you to the process to re-verify it under a new email address.

If you do have a duplicate page, go to my section on troubleshooting for tips on dealing with this.

If you DO NOT have a Google Local/Places/Maps page created for you already, you will have a blank slate. This is your opportunity to go through and fill out all the information.

Don't just fill out the information that's required. Fill out every single field. Ideally your target should be to get your account to 100% completeness.

How do you know if you are at 100%? When you log in to "Edit This Business Listing", under "Business Info", there is a scrubber bar that tells you the percentage towards complete that you are. This bar is located on your dashboard at www.google.com/places at the top of the page on the right hand side. It will tell you the percentage complete. This needs to be at a 100%. If it's not, then you are not ranking as high as you could. Rarely do I see a Google Local listing that has 100% completeness. It is an easy thing to do. You just have to take the time to do it.

You will need several pieces of basic information. For example:

- your country
- company name on your sign or business license
- physical address
- phone number

 It is widely thought that Google sorts their databases by phone number. Using a consistent phone number on all of your Google Local pages and other directory listings will have an impact on how well your Google Local listing ranks.

- email address
- website - ensuring that you have a link to your website is important. Further ensuring that your website has a good quality score is also important.

 Google Insiders say: Some of the ranking of your Google Local listing has to do with the Search Engine Optimization (SEO) of the website that is linked to the listing.

If there is a website linked to the Google Local page, you can bet that Google's spiders are indexing it and correlating the information. This gives Google a better picture of the business.

Once you gather all of the above information, you're ready to start.

Description

Always fill out the description area knowing that it is keyword-sensitive. A good tactic is to have this area full of keywords weaved into sentences describing your business. This is one of the first things that people are going to read. So be sure the sentences will speak to your customer. What is the single biggest benefit to doing business with you versus one of your competitors? Put it here. Although you can put keywords separated by commas (a.k.a.: keyword stuffing), there are other areas you can do this that the public won't see as often.

Ensure that visitors can see what the company offers in the description field. It is much easier for a visitor to see your services in the description field than in the category field.

Many people get the description and category fields confused. They serve two different purposes. The description field is telling consumers what the company is all about. If there are other services not listed in the auto populated categories, then you'll want to ensure that you put them in the description field.

You should creatively add as many keywords as possible into a sentence. Obviously, just like SEO the more keywords you have the better. Unlike regular SEO, you can get a little bit more direct.

Categories

The category field is telling Google where this page should show up. Though visitors can see the categories, many times they are truncated, which means, visitors will only see the first one.

This is also a futuristic tool for semantic search. In the very near future, you will be able into speak to your phone about what you want. Instead of going to a search engine and typing in, "Dallas private scuba diving lessons", you'll be able to speak into your phone saying "Dallas scuba diving instructor". It's called semantic search and it will change the way we search the internet. Google has setup the category field in advance of the semantic search phenomenon.

Regardless, the rule is to always fill out as many categories as possible. Right now, you can only fill out five. <u>One of those has to be a designated auto populated category.</u> For example, when you start typing in "scuba", the category "dive shop" will auto-populate. It is a pre-set category. You must have one true Google category. The other four can be custom categories.

The Most Important Detail to Remember When Setting up a Category

Remember, this is all about semantic search. It has to fit into the following statement; "this place is a (insert description here)".Google is specifically looking for the category keywords to be structured in this way. For example, you would not say "this place is a scuba dive". You would say "this place is a scuba diving instructor", or "this place scuba rental shop" or "this place is a swim lessons center". This is incredibly important because if you do not fit into

Google's particular phrasing, it could be marked as category spam. Worse yet, their software might misinterpret your page.

Since the categories are so important, I will elaborate on the auto-populate feature. When you are filling in the category field, it will provide pre-populated categories that Google already has programmed into the algorithm. If I type in "lawyer" the category "attorney" auto populates. In a separate category, I can include "lawyer". That is ensuring that I have at least one Google-appropriate category. The other categories are designed to describe the first category more. For instance, if you list "attorney" as your auto-populated category, in the other categories you can fill in what type of attorney you are, what type of legal services you provide.

Bottom line: always make sure that your categories are either auto-populated by Google, or phrased in a way that allows Google to read them.

Attention Many times when the information has not been updated or the information is correct on the back end but not on the customer facing side, it is because there has been some sort of pause placed on the account. This could be for either category spam or spam. In my experience, nine times out of ten, when a page is not showing it is due to some type of unintentional spam.

Service Areas and Location Settings

How to Hide Your Address if You Work From home

This can be a big issue for businesses that do not want the potential harassment from customers. If you work at home or have a business that just has a P.O. Box and no physical store front, then list the address where you receive mail on your listing. Often that is the home address.

If you do not want your address to show up - but you do want to service a certain area - then click, "Yes, this business serves customers at their locations". Next, click this check box, "Do not show my business address on my maps listing".

Now you can offer a service area custom designed by you. For example, the service area for your company could be a 20-mile radius (40-mile diameter) from your zip code. You can choose individual zip codes, or you could select a city to serve. The Google Local interface is intelligent enough to create a service area based on the areas that you type in.

Your home business will show up in searches for any of the areas you input into the service area. However, there will not be any clients or customers that see your home address. This will help home businesses that do not want customers showing up at their home address during dinner time.

A trick that I use based on my feedback from Google is to use a zip code of the area I want to promote. For example, if you are in the north part of town, but want to promote yourself in an area of the city that is more central, use the zip code of the area you want to promote. When Google sends their confirmation card, 99% of the time it will still come to the right address even with an incorrect zip code.

It's a great strategy for the businesses that work at the customer's site like plumbers, locksmiths, and HVAC. They are sometimes set up in shops on the outskirts of town, making their physical zip code further away from where they really conduct most of their business.

 The Google Local pages that perform the best have a physical address listed. The reason being, Google Local is designed to help people find local businesses.

Hours of Operation

You Are Always Open

Business Hours: Sometimes I hear from people that there are not operating hours for their business. Understandably, not all businesses have operating hours. Nonetheless, if your business has hours, it is essential that you include them in the Google Local setup. It is extremely important now because there is an option in the mobile app that says, "Only show me businesses that are open now." The bottom line, if you do not have hours listed, then your listing is not going to show up.

Payment Options

Your Listing is Almost 100% Complete

Payment options: This may not sound like a big deal, but it is going to get your page to 100% completeness. To iterate, when your account is at 100% completeness, it is going to be weighted heavier, and shown more frequently.

Photos and Videos

Adding photos and videos: This is simple. To do this, simply click "Add Photo" or "Add video". Find them on your computer and upload them into the Google Local interface. The same applies to videos. You can literally link to any YouTube video that you have the rights to. If you have a YouTube account with a bunch of videos on there, then pick the top five and include the YouTube link.

You can have up to ten photos and five videos. You can go to istockphoto.com and get some industry-generic photos to include. People like to do business with people, not trucks or logos. Include a picture of the owner and your click through rate will typically be above average. Use the pictures or videos to communicate the culture and the services.

Ideas for photos include: logo, office view from the street, smiling staff members, staff members at work, staff members collaborating with one another, the owners, vehicle with logo on it, or business pet. This part of the page is one of the biggest determining factors in success. There is a direct correlation between more pictures and more activity.

Photos and videos add more depth to the page and the click through rates are better.

I have seen significant value through increased click through rates by including the top 5 Frequently Asked Questions (FAQ). You can use a flip cam or cell phone. Ask the business owner to answer those 5 FAQs questions then upload them to YouTube.

YouTube has an easy-to-use editor tool that allows you to add text into any video. In the example of the 5 FAQs, you could add in a title card that has the question. Then upload the business owner answering the question. It allows the potential customer to begin building trust before they even pick up the phone.

Attention: Don't link to a video that you don't have permission to. If it gets flagged, it will cause the entire Google Local page to be pulled down. Not only that, but YouTube has a three-strikes-and-you're-out policy.

Additional Details

Many times, the users will not see this category because it will not always show up. It is important to note that Google does see it. This is a great place to include all kinds of keywords.

You could include every single service that your dive shop offers and then write something short, but descriptive, to the side. This is a great way to get some extra keywords on your page so that the spiders can see your services. However, it is not necessary to get to 100% completeness.

I have a customer that teaches swim lessons. One day he asked, "What should I put in the Additional Details section?" I said, "Well, you guys cater to all skill levels. You could put in the first column beginners swim lessons. Then in the second column list all the levels of beginners swim lessons that you offer; for example, pike, polliwog, guppy. If someone is searching for a particular level of beginners swim lessons in Austin, Texas, odds are you are the only person that is running Google Local listing on a particular swim certification in the Austin area. Now click through and submit this. You will likely see two different verification options. You are going to be asked to verify by phone or by postcard. You will want to have access to a direct line; not a line with an extension tree on it. When Google calls that phone number, you should be able to pick up the phone and answer it directly. If you can do this, then click "by phone."

Be sure that you are there at the phone or make sure that you call someone at the phone. Have that person write down that 5-digit pin number. Google is going to call you immediately after clicking the "by phone" verification option. The receiver of the call is going to get a 5-digit pin. You should be able to type in that 5-digit pin to complete the verification process.

In the instance of a new account, Google is not going to give you the phone verification option. It is going to ask for postcard verification. Your only option is to click the "postcard" option. When it arrives it will look similar to this.

GOO OUT OF GOOGLE

Google

Hello from Google,

You're almost done registering your business with Google.

After you verify your identity, your listing will go live in about a day. Then you can easily:

- Keep your hours, website, and other details up to date.
- Stand out with photos, videos, even coupons.
- View your personalized business dashboard for stats on who's visiting your listing and requesting directions to you.

Your business listing is:
Dr. Seuss
4407 Your Street
West Urban Area
TX
78 123

Customers like to know what's going on right now. Log in frequently to keep your information current and to check your latest stats on your business dashboard.

To verify your identity:

Step 1:
Go to www.google.com/local/add

Step 2:
To sign in, use your password and Google Account ID

Step 3:
Enter your PIN in the field next to your business listing and click Go.

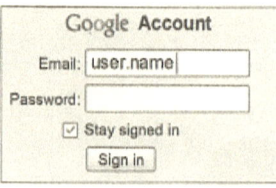
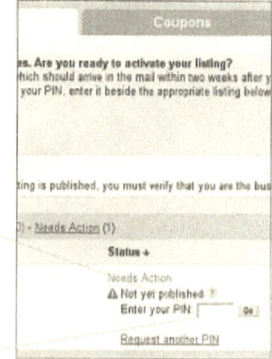

Your Pin is: **12345**

For more information, click "Google Places Help" at the bottom of www.google.com/local/add

Reviews

Having reviews is powerful. It not only provides more text for Google spiders to crawl, but often reviews are SEO-rich because customers are talking about the services that they had at your office.

As mentioned earlier, the reviews have recently changed in an incredible way. Now, when you're signed into Google and looking for a review, Google will show you reviews from people you know first. Obviously, you're going to tend to believe a review from someone you know as opposed to someone you aren't familiar with. You trust the people you're interacting with more. This is an incredible piece of technology that is only going to grow in importance.

So not only are reviews one of the most important factors for your business, but they will continue to grow in importance in the future. Bottom line: get more reviews on your Google Local page.

A review with a higher score will help your page rank better than one with a lower score.

To capture more reviews, a recommended strategy is to have a Google Local badge on your website that links to your Google page. Somewhere around the icon, in text, you could say "Tell us about your experience". Again, that icon should link directly to the Google Local page where they can write a review. You can also hand out business cards that have a photo of your business on one side and on the other side say, "Please tell us about your experience."

Driving traffic to the Google Local page and getting customers to select the star ratings is fine. For your customers to write a fully-developed idea of what they thought the business was, what they thought could be done better, and what they love about it will give your Google Local page a better ranking. Conversely, if the passion that you have for your business shows through in responding to a negative review, it is exponentially more valuable for future potential customers to see that than it is to have somebody put a 5-star review that says, "Food is great."

Sometimes it is better to have a rating of 10 coupled with a keyword-rich, long review than it is to just have one 20-point review that has no wording whatsoever.

Responding to Negative Reviews Easy

What to say
What to avoid saying?
Who are you writing to?

Use too many keywords and your review may be ranked as quality content. You certainly do not want to bring any more attention to the negative review.

First, understand that you are *not* talking to the person who wrote the review. You are talking to potential customers who may be reading the review later down the road.

An owner can (and should) respond to any review. Within the Google dashboard, there is a tab that says "Respond to reviews." Click it. Now you can scroll down to all of the reviews and respond publicly as the owner. How should you respond? Use this simple checklist below.

5-Point Checklist for Responding to Reviews

Quite often, business owners call me asking, "How can I remove a negative review?" Removing that review is nearly impossible. The best thing that you can do is to respond to the review. Again, remember your audience. You are not talking to the person who wrote the review, you are talking to the future customers who will be making a decision about your business while reading the review. Use the following points to help you craft a solid response.

1. Is the review true?
2. If yes, what did you do to rectify the issue?
3. If no, what makes you think it is untrue?
4. If this were to happen today, what would be done differently?
5. Have a neutral person read the review to ensure it is not too emotional.

GOO OUT OF GOOGLE

Everyone makes mistakes. Everyone has customers that they just can't keep happy. If you follow this checklist, your reviews will look like they were written by a customer service pro.

When responding to a review, keywords are weighted heavily. Try to use as few keywords as possible.

Duplicate Pages

If you have duplicate pages and have tried to remove some/all of them, but still continue to see the old page, it could be a matter of timing. For example, some of the pages could still be cached somewhere on a server that you have no control over. Until a new index push is created, your old version of the page will not be erased. In a situation where there are duplicate pages and many of them share the same address, the server is trying to cluster the pages all together.

This has created a confusing situation for Google's computers. It is a known issue and Google is working on it. Remember, we are working on Google time. Google's policy gives them 30 days to respond to a review. They try to do an index push every 3 weeks. This means that a normal response time could be as long as 51 days.

You could also have multiple listings in the same Google Local account for the same business location. If this is the case it is recommended that you make sure you have all the content backed up from the listing you will keep. Make sure the listing you want to keep is "active". Choose "Remove the listing from my Google Places account" option. This will delete the other listings that you don't want. Google-time for this can be several weeks.

Can you imagine if your business took weeks, or even 51 days to respond to a complaint? You would be out of business. On the other side, you also charge your customers. Google does not. It is free.

Conclusion, if you didn't charge anyone, you could probably take 51 days to respond to their requests too.

Be patient. Google wants to respond to you.

ND# Troubleshooting

My listing is not showing as frequently as I would like.

Brand new listings sometimes will have a 90-day demotion period. Google wants to ensure sure that this is a legitimate business, that this information is correct.

My page is not showing. What can I do to get into the rotation more?

First, make sure your page is 100% complete. Has it been complete for 90 days? Google will give you page a 90-day demotion period while it evaluates your authenticity. Can you blame them? You could be a meth dealer selling out of your closet. They want to ensure that pages like the meth dealers don't get ranked.

Second, are your categories and description properly filled out? If not, you could be marked for category spam.

Attention There are several main areas that get flagged for spam. The first one is the company organization name. If you have something in the company organization name that is different from what reads on your business license, then it is going to get marked as category spam.

As a general rule, you cannot have anything in the company organization field that is not exactly how it reads on the sign on your door, on your business cards, and on your business license. The same applies to your address.

Third, on the second address line, many businesses have included things like "best dive shop in Miami", or "biggest store on rodeo drive", or "the big blue store at sun ridge mall. I have even seen people try to put keywords in this field. This is not what Google is looking for here. Opinions are more likely to get questioned and could possibly get flagged. The only thing that you might want to indicate in the second field is if this store was located inside a building or inside a mall. In that case you could in parentheses put "at Sun Ridge Mall."

My map marker is not in the correct place

Log into your Google Local account. Go to the user interface indicated by an icon that says "Business Owner". Click on "edit my page". Underneath the map, click on "Fix Incorrect Marker Location." Scroll up to the top. That will open a dynamic window that allows you to literally pick up the map marker and move it. Now click "save changes". Scroll back down to the bottom and click "submit". Your map marker has been changed.

I did everything you said and I'm still not showing

Did you wait 60 days? Remember, Google's literature shows that a 51 day response time is normal. Often times, a change will reflect on the back-end server, but will not be pushed to the live server until Google has a large index push. Google is trying to do a new push every 3-4 weeks.

Try giving it 60 days, if it still doesn't rank, go to the end of this book, go to my website, get my phone number, and call me. I will be happy to give you a free consultation.

get an error saying, "We Currently Do Not Support the Location"

Much has been written about this. All I can say is that technology is great, when it works. This is a bug. As of press time, Google hasn't

GOO OUT OF GOOGLE

fixed this yet. Suffice it to say that Google insiders tell me it can happen for any number of reasons including merged listings, old servers not refreshing their cached pages, duplicate listings, etc...

If you get this error, my suggestion is to plan on this process taking twice as long. You will need to be diligent and patient. The other option is to delegate / hire someone to do that for you.

Closing

Believe it or not, you know more about creating an effective Google listing than the majority of your competitors. The majority of your competition is too busy working for their business instead of working on their business. For that, I congratulate you. The tips, tricks and methodologies I've shared with you in Taking the Goo Out of Google Local are the same that online marketing consultants would use if you paid them 50 times the amount you paid for this book. Now, you can use them yourself and reap what you sow.

Remember, do not pull up the flowers to find out how the roots are growing. You will need to live on Google time to get the promised harvest. The secret is to ensure your listing is setup 100% complete and that the text is written in a way that Google can read it.

I'm sincerely appreciative of the interest you've expressed by reading this book. It is likely that I do not know you, although we may have met in my Taking the Goo Out of Google workshops, or perhaps we've done business together. Regardless, I hope this has helped to increase your understanding and commitment to implement a better presence online. To request a free consultation or additional information about Steve Huskey's online marketing program or other products and services, please call 512.590.5957. You can also email StevenHuskey@gmail.com. Please keep me posted on how the ideas in this book have helped you.

www.ingramcontent.com/pod-product-compliance
Lightning Source LLC
Chambersburg PA
CBHW021850170526
45157CB00006B/2387